Always By Your Side

A GUIDED JOURNAL
OF 75 TREASURES
FROM MOMMY TO DAUGHTER

This Journal Belongs to

.....

Inspiration

· · · · ·

We always love picking the brains and memories of influential people in our lives, giving us insight into our shared history or a nuanced perspective of the world around us. These journals help create a space for children of all ages to learn from and about their parents in a personal and meaningful way.

Included with the prompts are coloring pages, creative writing areas, and more! This series was inspired by an amazing colleague when we were both youth coordinators for a non-profit. One of the many, many things we loved about her was her open communication and the strong relationships she built the students in the programs as well as with her own children. After she lost her battle with cancer, we considered the unanswered questions her children, and countless others have during momentous occasions, when a loved one passes.

We resolved that when we had children we would strive to have conversations with them to answer these questions. Fast forward to our first child. I began a journal for her when she was born. I wrote about the fun things I observed her doing, the funny things she would say, as well as the conversations I wanted to have with her in the future. Thinking of our friend, I also began to write about topics, events, and experiences our daughter may encounter in the future. Those ideas were compiled into this journal resource to help parents build strong relationships and leave a legacy of wisdom and comfort for their children.

When I was
a little girl,
I *used to*
love to play

Date_____

_____

_____

_____

_____

_____

_____

_____

_____

_____

_____

_____

_____

_____

_____

_____

_____

_____

_____

_____

_____

When you were
a toddler, I
laughed
hysterically
when you

Date

A true friend will always

Date _____

_____
_____
_____
_____

_____
_____
_____
_____
_____
_____
_____
_____
_____
_____
_____
_____
_____
_____
_____
_____
_____
_____
_____

I look at you
with wonder
and amazement
that

Date _____

_____

_____

_____

_____

_____

_____

_____

_____

_____

_____

_____

_____

_____

_____

_____

_____

_____

_____

_____

On your
first day
of school

Date _____

_____
_____
_____

_____

_____

_____

_____

_____

_____

_____

_____

_____

_____

_____

_____

_____

_____

_____

_____

_____

My top five favorite favorite songs are

Date

Here's a funny
story from my
childhood

Date

A gentleman should always

Date_____

_____

_____

_____

"No" is a complete
sentence. "No."
always means no
and this is what
I mean

Date_____

I *would use these*
three powerful
adjectives to
describe you

Date

_____

_____

_____

_____

_____

_____

_____

_____

_____

_____

_____

_____

_____

_____

_____

_____

_____

_____

_____

_____

_____

_____

_____

Some of my favorite ways to give back are

Date

To me, love looks like

Date_____

_____

_____

_____

After high school, I chose to

Date _____

_____

_____

_____

My three
favorite
books are

Date _____

_____
_____
_____

Here's an interesting story about your Dad

Date

I've
always
dreamed of

Date_____

Self-care is important. Here are some ways I enjoy practicing self-care.

Date _____

*You need to
know this
about boys*

Date

*On your
journey to
becoming wise,
remember to*

Date_____

_____

_____

_____

*Here are some
girly tips that
people may not
tell you about*

Date_____
_____
_____
_____
_____
_____
_____
_____
_____
_____
_____
_____
_____
_____
_____
_____
_____
_____
_____
_____
_____
_____

My
favorite
place to
visit is

Date _____

_____
_____
_____

When your
body starts
to change

Date

As a grown-up, my favorite thing to do with my family is

Date

Here's the
secret
recipe to

Date_____

_____

_____

_____

_____

_____

_____

_____

_____

_____

_____

_____

_____

_____

_____

_____

_____

_____

_____

_____

_____

_____

_____

When I am sad,
this is what I do to
make sure I don't
stay in a sad space
for long

Date _____

A true
friend
will never

Date _____

_____

_____

_____

Some things that life taught me that I never learned in school

Date

When I was
younger, I
remember getting
in trouble for

Date

_____

_____

_____

_____

_____

_____

_____

_____

_____

_____

_____

_____

_____

_____

_____

_____

_____

_____

_____

_____

_____

_____

How you should act when you lose or when you win

Date

_____

_____

_____

_____

_____

_____

_____

_____

_____

_____

_____

_____

_____

_____

_____

_____

_____

_____

_____

_____

_____

Your first
co-ed party
by yourself,
remember to

Date _____

_____

_____

_____

Did you know I used to

Date

I *love this*
about you

Date

*I remember
the
time you*

Date_____
_____
_____
_____

_____
_____
_____
_____
_____
_____
_____
_____
_____
_____
_____
_____
_____
_____
_____
_____
_____
_____

I *have*
always enjoyed
movies that

Now that
you're a
teenager

Date

Some of my favorite beauty secrets are

Date _____

*Don't be
afraid to*

Date

It's your first
homecoming
and I'm so excited
to tell you

Date

*Even if a
man can do it,
a lady should
always know
how to*

Date_____

_____
_____
_____
_____

_____
_____
_____
_____
_____
_____
_____
_____
_____
_____
_____
_____
_____
_____
_____
_____
_____
_____

If I could
have a super
power, it
would be

Date _____
_____
_____
_____

Traits you should value in the person you'd want to be your significant other

Date _____

One thing
that used to
bother me but
doesn't
anymore is

Date

On your first date, I want you to remember

Date _____

_____

_____

_____

_____

_____

_____

_____

_____

_____

_____

_____

_____

_____

_____

_____

_____

_____

_____

_____

_____

_____

Everybody
makes mistakes.
When you
mess up

Date

Some things that I learned in school that I actually used in real life

Date

Breaking up
often feels
bad; however

I hope you always remember the time when we

Date_____

_____

_____

_____

_____

_____

_____

_____

_____

_____

_____

_____

_____

_____

_____

_____

_____

_____

_____

_____

_____

My favorite
vacation with
you was

Date

On your

Sweet 16

Date _____

_____

_____

_____

Growing up being an only child, youngest child, middle child, or oldest child (circle one) was

Date _____

_____

_____

_____

_____

_____

_____

_____

_____

_____

_____

_____

_____

_____

_____

_____

_____

_____

_____

_____

_____

_____

_____

You know you've found true love when

Date _____

_____

_____

_____

Is *it time for your driver's license already? Always remember to*

Date_____

_____

_____

_____

The first
time I lived
on my own, I

Date_____

_____
_____
_____

_____
_____
_____
_____
_____
_____
_____
_____
_____
_____
_____
_____
_____
_____
_____
_____

On your prom night, I want you to know

Date_____

_____
_____
_____

What I loved about my first car was

Date _____

_____

_____

_____

_____

_____

_____

_____

_____

_____

_____

_____

_____

_____

_____

_____

_____

_____

_____

_____

_____

_____

_____

Growing up, my favorite thing to do with my family was

Date

When in doubt

Date _____

_____

_____

_____

When you ride a bus or a plane, remember to

Date_____

_____

_____

_____

_____

_____

_____

_____

_____

_____

_____

_____

_____

_____

_____

_____

_____

_____

_____

_____

_____

_____

On the day of your graduation

Date

The best part of being your Mom is

Date_____
_____
_____
_____
_____
_____
_____
_____
_____
_____
_____
_____
_____
_____
_____
_____
_____
_____
_____
_____
_____

If you ever
feel down
on your luck,
remember

Date

*On your
wedding day,
I want you
to know*

Date _____

_____

_____

_____

No matter how wealthy you become, always remember

Date_____

_____

_____

_____

Here are a
few tips to
nail that
interview

Date_____

_____

_____

_____

In school, I
was really
good at

Date_____

_____

_____

_____

_____

_____

_____

_____

_____

_____

_____

_____

_____

_____

_____

_____

_____

_____

_____

_____

_____

_____

_____

_____

My
grandparents
used to
always
tell me

Date _____

_____

_____

_____

_____

What I learned from my first job

Date_____

_____

_____

_____

_____

_____

_____

_____

_____

_____

_____

_____

_____

_____

_____

_____

_____

_____

_____

_____

_____

Celebrating the birth of your baby, I want you to know

Date_____

_____

_____

_____

Here are my definitions for "failure" and "success"

Date

_____

_____

_____

_____

_____

_____

_____

_____

_____

_____

_____

_____

_____

_____

_____

_____

_____

_____

_____

_____

When it comes
to religion
and spirituality,
I feel like

Date

My two favorite quotes are

*One person
who has
significantly
influenced my
life is*

Date

My
parents used
to tell me

Date

Now that
you're a
Mommy

Date _____

_____
_____
_____

Growing up,
my siblings
and I
used to

Date_____

_____

_____

_____

_____

_____

_____

_____

_____

_____

_____

_____

_____

_____

_____

_____

_____

_____

_____

_____

_____

_____

I want you to always know how proud I am of you and

Date _____

_____

_____

_____

_____

_____

_____

_____

_____

_____

_____

_____

_____

_____

_____

_____

_____

_____

_____

_____

_____

Free Write

.....

Now that you've got the hang of it, use the following pages to write about topics more specific to you and your family, go into more detail about something previously discussed, or let your daughter ask you some questions that have sparked her curiosity.

Date_____

Date

Date_____

Date

Date_____

Date

Date_____

Date_____

Date

Date_____

Family Tree

On the next page, you can map out your family tree. Use the circles to write your family members' names and use the lines to write how they are related to you. See the example below for an idea of how to complete your own. There's no right or wrong way. Have fun! Be creative!

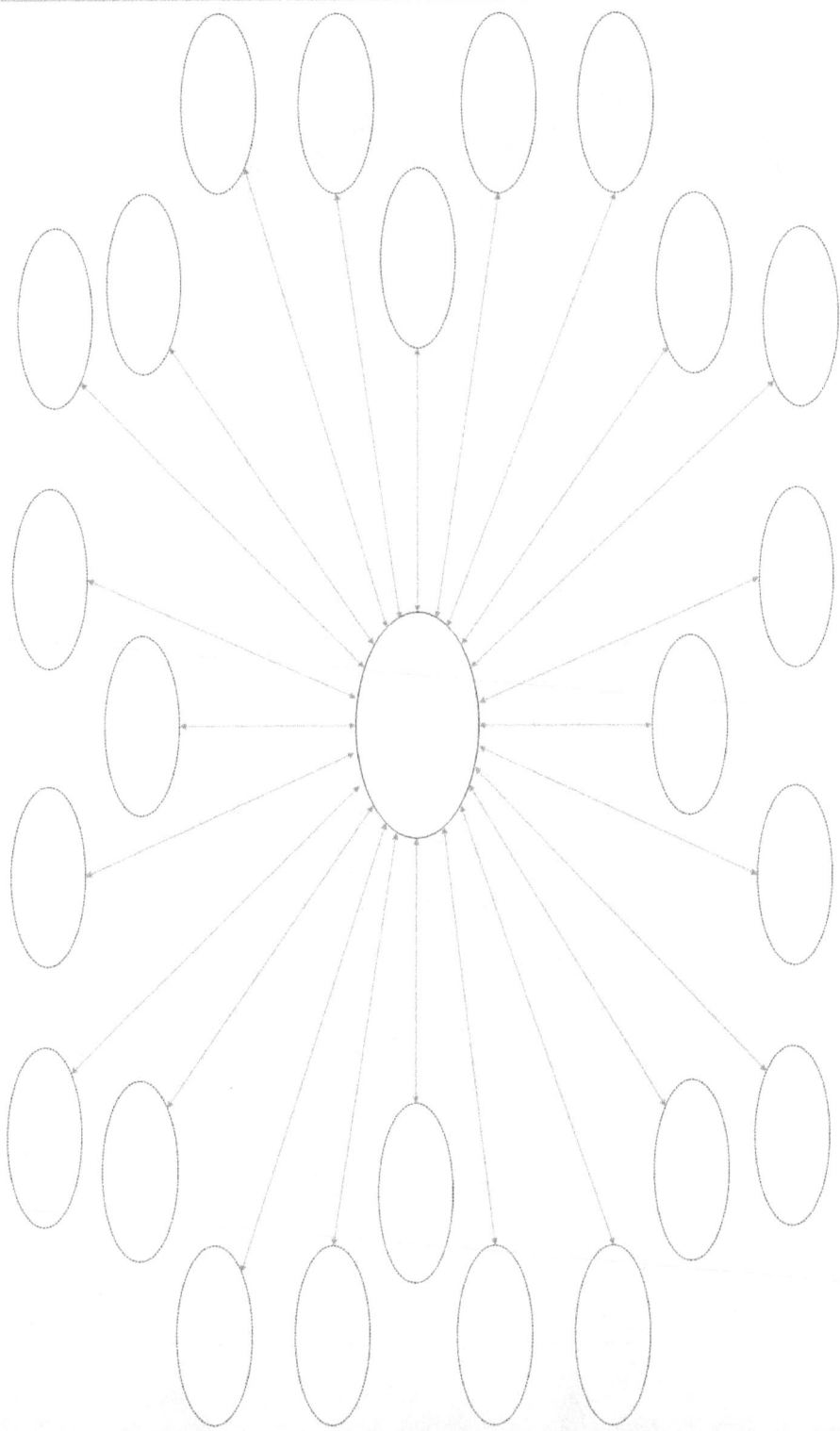

You and Me

. . . . .

Full Name

Birthdate

Birth Weight

Full Name

Birthdate

Birth Weight

Picture of Us